D1685268

Izzi Howell

800844126

Franklin Watts

First published in paperback in Great Britain in 2022 by The Watts Publishing Group

Copyright © The Watts Publishing Group, 2018

Produced for Franklin Watts by
White-Thomson Publishing Ltd
www.wtpub.co.uk

ISBN: 978 1 4451 5961 4

10 9 8 7 6 5 4 3 2 1

Credits

Series Editor: Izzi Howell
Series Designer: Rocket Design (East Anglia) Ltd
Designer: Clare Nicholas
Literacy Consultant: Kate Ruttle

The publisher would like to thank the following for permission to reproduce their pictures: Alamy: Friedrich Stark 16; Getty: aluxum cover, AlpamayoPhoto 7t, CRSHELARE 9t, Lysogor 10, Danielrao 11, ShashikantDurshettiwar 15t, GOH CHAI HIN/AFP 17, anshu18 18r, Nikada 19t, hadynyah 19b, ewastudio 21t; Shutterstock: turtix title page and 12, Alfonso de Tomas 4, pavalena 5t, railway fx 5b, saiko3p 6t, 6b and 7b, Sam Dcruz 8, Scorpp 9b, Sumit.Kumar.99 13, espies 14 and 22, Jamie Rogers 15b, SMDSS 18l, Dmytro Gilitukha 20, Eric Isselee 21b.

Every attempt has been made to clear copyright. Should there be any inadvertent omission please apply to the publisher for rectification.

Printed in Dubai

Franklin Watts
An imprint of
Hachette Children's Group
Part of The Watts Publishing Group
Carmelite House
50 Victoria Embankment
London EC4Y 0DZ

An Hachette UK Company
www.hachette.co.uk
www.franklinwatts.co.uk

All words in **bold** appear in the glossary on page 23.

Contents

Where is India?

India is a **country** in **Asia**.

India is in the south of Asia.
▼

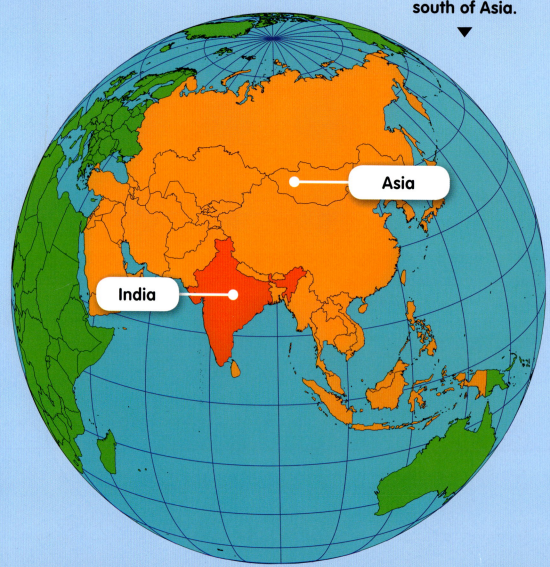

Asia

India

AFGHANISTAN

PAKISTAN

CHINA

DELHI

NEPAL

Agra

BHUTAN

•Jodhpur

Ganges

INDIA

BANGLADESH

MYANMAR

•Mumbai

Indian Ocean

SRI LANKA

◀ **The coast of India is on the Indian Ocean.**

India is a large country. It is next to other countries, such as Pakistan and Bangladesh.

This is the flag of India. ▶

Cities

Delhi is the **capital city** of India. This is where the Indian **government** works.

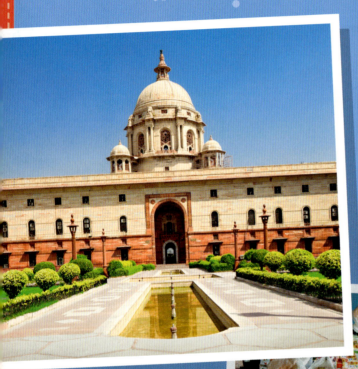

◀ The **president** of India lives in this house in Delhi.

This shop in Delhi sells colourful **spices**. ▶

There are many other cities in India. Mumbai is the biggest city in the country.

Boats come to the harbour in Mumbai.
▼

▲ **Many buildings are painted blue in the city of Jodhpur.**

7

Countryside

There are tall mountains in the north of India. These mountains are called the Himalayas.

▼ These people have climbed to the top of a mountain in the Himalayas.

How would you feel at the top of a tall mountain?

Farmers grow **crops** such as tea and rice. Tea is grown on hills. Rice is grown on wet land near rivers.

These Indian women are planting rice. ▶

These hills in the north of India are covered in tea fields. ▼

Weather

Most of India has warm weather all year round. There are forests in wet areas where it often rains. Deserts have hot, dry weather.

The weather on the south coast of India is usually sunny.
▼

In the south of India, it rains
a lot from June to September.
This heavy rain is called
a monsoon.

When does
it rain where
you live?

▼ There are often **floods** during the monsoon season.

Interesting places

The Taj Mahal is a famous Indian building in the city of Agra. It was built by an **emperor** of India. It is nearly four hundred years old.

Millions of people visit the Taj Mahal every year. ▼

This huge **temple** is in Delhi. It is built in the shape of a lotus flower.

Find a picture of a lotus flower. How does the temple look like the flower?

▼ There are gardens around the temple.

Food

In India, people often eat vegetable or meat curries. Curries are made with many different spices.

Have you tried curry before? What type of curry was it?

People eat curry with bread or rice. This is chapati bread. ▶

◀ Gulab jamun are sweet balls soaked in syrup.

There are many types of Indian sweets. People eat sweets as desserts or on special occasions.

These sweets are called barfi. They are made from milk and pistachios. ▶

barfi

pistachios

Sport

Many people in India like cricket.
They watch cricket matches
on TV and at cricket grounds.

These boys are
playing cricket
in the street.
▼

Kabaddi is a **traditional** Indian sport. A player from one team tries to 'tag' players from the other team.

Kabaddi players can **tackle** the player from the other team. ▼

Would you rather play cricket or kabaddi?

Festivals

Some Indians **celebrate** Divali in October or November. Divali is a festival of light. People light lamps and candles.

People make decorations using coloured sand at Divali. ▶

A Divali lamp

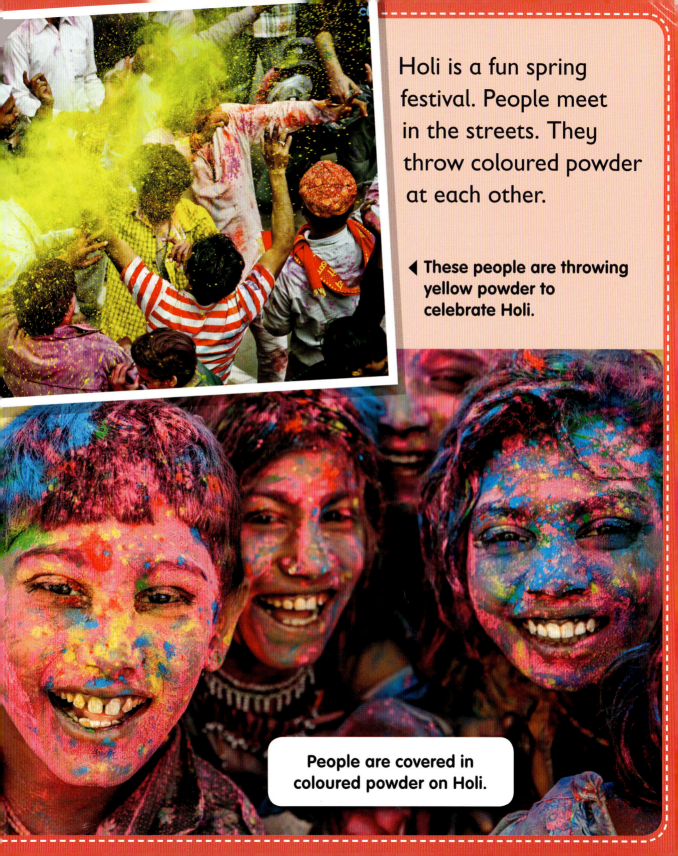

Holi is a fun spring festival. People meet in the streets. They throw coloured powder at each other.

◀ These people are throwing yellow powder to celebrate Holi.

People are covered in coloured powder on Holi.

Wildlife

Asian elephants live in **grasslands** and forests in India. They look for grass and leaves to eat.

In hot weather, elephants like to cool down in rivers and lakes.
▼

How do you cool down in hot weather?

◀ Tigers have sharp teeth to help them cut through meat.

There are tigers and snakes in forests in India. Sometimes, tigers come into towns and cities to look for food to eat.

The king cobra uses poison to catch animals to eat. ▶

Quiz

Test how much you remember.

Check your answers on page 24.

1 Name two countries that are next to India.

2 What is the largest city in India?

3 How old is the Taj Mahal?

4 What are gulab jamun?

5 When is Divali?

6 Where do elephants live in India?

Glossary

Asia – a continent that includes countries such as Japan, China and India

capital city – the city where a country's government works

celebrate – to do something fun on a special day

coast – land by the sea

country – an area of land that has its own government

crops – plants that we eat that are grown by farmers

emperor – a ruler who controls several countries

flood – when an area is covered in water

government – people who make the laws for a country

grassland – a large area of land covered in grass

harbour – a place where ships are kept, close to land

president – a leader of a country's government

spices – plants that give food a strong flavour

tackle – to stop someone from doing something in a sport

temple – a building where people go to pray or worship

traditional – describes something that has been done in the same way for many years

Index

Answers:

1: Pakistan, China, Nepal, Bangladesh, Myanmar, Bhutan; 2: Mumbai; 3: Nearly four hundred years old; 4: Sweet balls soaked in syrup; 5: October or November; 6: Grasslands and forests

Teaching notes:

Children who are reading Book band Purple or above should be able to enjoy this book with some independence. Other children will need more support.

Before you share the book:

- Show children different world maps and globes. Ensure they understand that blue represents sea and other colours show the land.
- Help them to orientate their understanding of the globe by pointing out where India is in relation to other countries they know of.
- Talk about what they already know about India and Asia.

While you share the book:

- Help children to read some of the more unfamiliar words.

- Talk about the questions. Encourage children to make links between their own experiences and the information in the book.
- Compare the information about India with where you live. What is the same? What is different?

After you have shared the book:

- Talk about the buildings shown in the pictures. How are they the same as, or different from, buildings where you live?
- Together, make a list of everything you can learn from the book about Indian landscape.
- If children in the class have friends or relations who have lived in India, ask them to talk to the children about what it is like to be there.
- Work through the free activity sheets at www.hachetteschools.co.uk